Another Way

Also by Dale Turner:

Different Seasons: Twelve Months of Wisdom & Inspiration

Grateful Living

DALE TURNER

Another Way

Open-Minded Faithfulness

HIGH
TIDE
PRESS
2000

A High Tide Book

Published by High Tide Press Inc.

3650 West 183rd Street, Homewood, Illinois 60430

Turner, Rev. Dale E. Another Way / by Dale Turner — 1st ed.

ISBN 1-892696-14-2

Printed in the United States of America

Book design by Alex Lubertozzi and Diane J. Bell

First Edition

Printed on acid-free paper.

We do not know what each new day will bring,
for God does not permit us to see over the hills
or around the corners. For some, the uncertainty
of the future brings fear and apprehension.
The best answer for them is the realization
that the future comes one day at a time.
—Dale E. Turner

appily, we do not move into the future alone. No matter what our need, there will usually be someone near to lend a hand. We live and move and have our being in God's presence. We are not orphans in an empty world.

✦

There is nothing more certain than uncertainty.

✦

I sometimes think I could get a lot done if I didn't have so many other things to do.

✦

There are reassurances in the midst of fragmented days. A consciousness of incompleteness is essential to a rational view of life as a whole. The real is always a fragment of the ideal; and the greater one's ideal, the more fragmentary the real sometimes appears. And the more we try to do, or the better we try

to become, the greater will be our consciousness
of fragmentation and incompleteness.

✦

No matter how long we live, we will all leave more
undone than we have ever been able to accomplish.

✦

The obvious necessity for bringing meaning
to the interruptions and the fragmented bits and
pieces of days and . . .of our lives, is to place them
in a framework constructed of patience, perseverance,
good humor, vision, caring and concern, with just
enough flexibility to notice and perhaps to follow a
new direction some interruption may be leading us.

✦

If we are honest with ourselves, we will admit that we
all hold prejudices . . . we are not born
with prejudices—we acquire them. . . from the family
and the society in which we live. . . Those who see
the fallacy of . . . prejudice make ours a brighter,
better and more just and loving world.

✦

The characteristics that we admire in human
nature grow best in a soil mixed with trouble.
Without hardship there would be no hardihood.
Without calamity there would be no courage.
Without trouble there would be
no triumphant living. . .

(Many) do not endure in the midst of privation
and disappointment—they prevail.

†∾†

It is a mark of high purpose to desire an intelligent
faith. It is not easy to come by. If we inherit our
faith, borrow it or swallow it without reflection,
it is not ours. Great faith . . . must be fought for.

†∾†

Contrary to what many believe, doubt is not
the opposite of faith, it is an element of faith.

†∾†

Often the religious man believes,
not because he finds his faith easy,
but because he finds its opposite incredible.

†∾†

We often condemn most violently in others those sins
which we should like to have committed ourselves.

†∾†

Humans stay alive by growing—by being born again
over and over each day, leaving behind a lesser being
and striving each day to be better than before. . .
Life is a series of rebirths and the challenge is not to
die before we are fully born.

†∾†

Why, in a world that cries for unity, must we go on
stressing the differences, and leave unexpressed
the countless ways we could join hand-in-hand
to bring in the day of justice, order and peace
for which we all yearn.

✛

Heaven begins on earth for those who are unselfish
and caring, who are sensitive to beauty both in nature
and in human life, and who live with a consciousness
of God's continuous presence.

✛

The meaning of the Resurrection . . . (is) that life in
God is endless and unconquerable . . . Jesus' way of
life (is) deathless and God's causes
are never lost causes, and there is a kind of life
that is endless on earth and beyond the grave.

✛

We give to others not only what we have and know,
but what we are.

✛

All strenuous living requires time-outs
—rest stops along the way. It is sometimes smart to be
"caught napping."

✛

The memory of the priceless gifts which have come
to us from those of other generations
is in itself a call to us to make our contributions
to the betterment of the world that is to be.

+∿+

A divided church that stands for something
is better than a united church that stands for nothing.

+∿+

We must guard ourselves against the poverty
of the mind that will not think,
the poverty of the heart that will not feel,
the poverty of the ears that will not hear and the eyes
that will not see. Those who awaken us to life's larger
joys are among our greatest benefactors.

+∿+

Love of self is an important religious teaching
because people cannot live amicably with others
unless they can live amicably with themselves.

+∿+

No one is only one self. We are many selves . . .
an important challenge in life, then, is to discover
our best self and nurture it so that it dominates
our life the maximum amount of time.

+∿+

There are countless worthy causes needing support.
In helping to heal the wounds of others,
we are helping to heal our own ills.

✛

Laughter is a tranquilizer with no side effects.
It is an instant vacation . . . Good humor is timeless.
It is like good art: if it is ever good, it is always good.

✛

Throughout history, human beings have used
"God's will" as the explanation for all things
which happened—good or bad—which they couldn't
explain. They have used it to condemn those things
which they did not like, or to promote those things
they did like. It is arrogant to presume that we
humans can always know the will of God.

✛

We should not glibly brand what we do not
understand, what we do not like or what we do like
as the will of God. It is important to think of God
aright, for we become like that which we worship.

✛

Mental and spiritual stagnation are the hazards
of middle age. It is then we should do as Mark Twain
suggested, "Take out your brain and jump on it. It
gets all caked up."

✛

Why is it that we are so reluctant to change—to grow?
It is not so much that new ideas are painful,
for they are not. It is that old ideas are
seldom false, but have truth,
even great truth . . .
but the danger (lies) in the process of putting all
thought and energy into preserving these values
(and so) we may miss the infinitely greater riches
which lie hidden in the future.

✛∿✛

It is a mark of maturity not to be
angered when another's interpretation
is not our own. Humble people do not
presume they have all the answers. . .
It is arrogant to expect others to share
all our conclusions . . . Lovers of liberty
must expect and even urge diversity.

✛∿✛

If we expect a trouble-free existence,
then any interruption of our tranquility
is an intruder to be resented. But if we see
trouble as an inevitable aspect of life,
even a prod to something finer, then it can
be turned to constructive ends.

✛∿✛

The mellowing and maturing effect that can come
when we suffer may make us better able to help others.

✛∿✛

The contribution of a mature religious faith
to the problem of pain and suffering lies not so much
in providing a theory to explain it as in furnishing a
power to surmount it.

✤

With a strong hub of faith, we can take a surprising
number of shocks and bumps on the outside rim
without sustaining permanent damage.

✤

The healthiest and most completely whole
and creative human beings are those who know
and practice what it is to give love
in nondemanding, non-manipulative ways.

✤

Love is the active power which enables us
to break through walls that separate us—
the doorway through which the human spirit moves
from solitude to society, from selfishness to service.

✤

To listen to another is to affirm that person,
and to enhance his or her sense of self-worth.

✤

The smallest good deed
is better than the grandest good intention.

✤

We must be willing, and even eager, in all of life,
to do more than is expected or required,
or we will always be average, mediocre, mundane
human beings.   The great personalities of history
have always . . . (given) more than was expected
or required and they (have always been)
ready to take less than they deserve.

↜↝

Be kinder than necessary.

↜↝

The generous giver is not determined
by how much is given, but by how much remains
after the gift is given.

↜↝

The life of a whole community is sometimes
transformed for good in its ideals and aims by people
who have never thought of themselves in terms of
trying to be an influence or deserving to be an
example.   But in the loyalty to their own highest
ideals, they walk steadily and constantly toward the
light of justice, honor and truth, and the shadow
of good influence falls behind them.   They attract
rather than compel others toward goodness, luring
them by the appeal of their own integrity and love.

↜↝

"We must do something," will always solve more
problems than "Something must be done."

+∿+

Choices are a part of the whole of life.
We live in an unfinished world. . . . We are
continuously shaping our own lives and the world
in which we live, by the choices we make.

+∿+

The dilemma of imperfect alternatives confronts us
because we do not live in a static, fixed world. We are
forever growing and changing . . . (and) we are finite
beings with limited knowledge.

+∿+

Only our relationship to God can ultimately rescue
us from our loneliness . . . . We are not alone.

+∿+

God has a purpose for each individual,
and no gift of mind or spirit is so small or useless
that it cannot be turned to a constructive end.

+∿+

Even the smallest hair casts its shadow.
Unless we do the work for which we were created,
our work will never be done.

+∿+

There are intangible gifts that . . . we can all afford
. . . the gift of praise and the gift of physical
presence. The two seem so simple and commonplace,
yet they are too often neglected or overlooked.

⇾◡↼

I have never seen a difference of opinion
as an occasion for estrangement.

⇾◡↼

People know that the one thing we have in common
is that we are all different. Lovers of liberty
must expect and even urge diversity.

⇾◡↼

We seldom learn anything
from someone who always agrees with us.

⇾◡↼

A life of faith is a ceaseless, unremitting quest—
a series of rebirths—each leading to a new discovery
and a new birth.

⇾◡↼

There is something of great integrity
and common sense in the willingness to work
with those with whom we do not always agree.

⇾◡↼

It is not ours to cast the stone of judgement,
but to offer the helping, healing hand of love
and reconciliation; it is not ours to assign blame,
but to accept responsibility for ourselves and to act
with charity toward others; it is not ours to proceed
self-righteously and vindictively, but to walk humbly,
penitently and searchingly toward the truth
that will truly set us free.

✦

There (is) no sin so small that Jesus will condone it,
nor any transgression he (will) not forgive.

✦

In Matthew 7:1-2, when
Jesus said, "Judge not, that you be not judged,"
he was alluding to the fact that every time
we judge someone or something, we are also
making a judgement on ourselves . . .
When we criticize a comment or an action
of another, we reveal who and what we are.

✦

The ability to evaluate, judge and decide carries with
it a responsibility to do so honestly and with love. It
is easier to be critical than to be correct and it is
difficult to be correct in our judgements.
For people do change.

✦

We (may) be held accountable, not only for our sins,
but for our failures to enjoy all of the legitimate
pleasures of this world.

꙳

Few of us have many great days in life.
Most of our days are commonplace and routine
. . . We live most in the appreciation and enjoyment
of the little joys that come and go almost unnoticed. . .
It is in appreciating and enjoying the life that is ours
that we live our prayer of gratitude with God.

꙳

In spite of the complexities of our fast moving
society, it is still possible to hear that still small voice
of conscience and to catch hold
of what is honest and true.

꙳

Life is not so much a matter of finely spun theories
as it is a matter of concrete tasks and everyday
responsibilities . . . We act our way
into right thinking more readily
than we think our way into right acting.

꙳

People do not believe in immortality
because they have proved it, but they are forever
trying to prove it because they believe it.

꙳

Eternal life begins not at the moment of physical
death, but at the moment of spiritual rebirth,
the moment of moving from a self-centered life
to a God-centered life.

✛

Love is the most powerful force in the world.

✛

Tender loving care and affirmation can both prevent
and heal physical disease and lift the human spirit
out of the ruts of mental illness and depression . . .
Those who practice love's power are lifted
above enmity and vindictiveness. They are set free
from the burden of grudges and hatreds.

✛

The experiences of many human beings has revealed
that trouble, while appearing as an unwelcome
intruder, may be a blessing in disguise.. .
Often, it is not at the hour of trouble, but only
in retrospect, that we see the positive values of the
problems we have encountered, and the hand
of God's leading. . .   There are no such things
as hard knocks without advantages.

✛

Each generation has its own responsibility and its own
challenge. What already has been accomplished
is but a prelude to that which is yet to be done.

✛

It is common sense to know that it is not always
possible to live amiably with everyone, nor is it wise.
The only people who agree with everyone
are those who have no ideas of their own.

❦

It is wise to take pleasure in the blessings and skills
of others. When we find someone who surpasses us,
be thankful that such gifts are in our midst,
a public banquet to which we are all invited. . .
The remedy to envy is to learn to accept one's self
and one's gifts, however modest, and to make
the best use of them to make a better world.

❦

God (holds us) accountable only for what we are
capable of becoming or doing. People are fools
not to be what they can because they can't be what
they think they want to be.

❦

The real measure of our wealth is how much we would
be worth if we lost all our money.

❦

Greed, which leads to excess, can blind us to the
needs of those who have not. It is possible to have so
much power that we become indifferent to the rights
and claims of others; to have so much health that we
do not understand the sick; . . . to have so many
material goods that we prize possessions more than

love and friendships . . . to have so much knowledge
that we become proud and self sufficient.

✦

Character is not a gift. It is a conquest.
And the kingdom of character always lies upstream.
It is never reached by drifting. It comes to those
who courageously battle the currents
and headwinds of temptations.

✦

Words vocalize thoughts, and the tongue
reveals what the mind is thinking. It is not
easy to bridle the tongue, but there is no
merit in saying everything that comes to mind.
It is wisdom to ask ourselves three questions
before commenting about another: Is it true?
Is it kind? Is it necessary?

✦

The atmosphere of a home is conditioned by spoken
words, and the grave of love is dug with little digs.

✦

It is a distortion of truth and justice
if we fail to be conscious of a person's virtues,
no matter how great the blot.

✦

When we believe that the days ahead will be good days,
we move forward with confidence and hope,
and by such positive outlook,
we help to fulfill our expectations.

✦

The optimist proclaims that we live in the best of all
possible worlds. The pessimist fears this is true.

✦

In looking out beyond the self to God, whose face has
been mirrored clearly in the great prophets,
in Jesus, and in religious leaders of many religions,
millions of people have been rescued from lesser
desires and have lived lives of great personal
satisfaction and helpfulness to others.

✦

If our spirits are growing, we experience
new enthusiasm and a deeper appreciation
for even small amenities—a smile, a hug, a handshake,
a meal, a bed, eyes to see, ears to hear,
friends and family to love—the list is endless.

✦

Those who aim to live courageously today must often
be willing to sacrifice momentary satisfactions
and endure relative hardships for the sake of worthy
goals and high causes.

✦

The mature person is honest enough to accept
personal responsibility for his wayward ways, and does
not search for a scapegoat devil to bear the blame.
Whether we think of the devil as a literal person
or a terrifying evil potency, or whether we think
of the devil as a symbolic word for the human tendency
to succumb to the lower trends of our nature will vary
with the individual's training and beliefs. It is really
not the most important thing. The important issue
is: "How do we respond in the hour of temptation?"

✦

Courage is the conquest of fear,
rather than the absence of it.

✦

Courage is mercy and forgiveness
when revenge would be sweet and timely
and would teach the other fellow a lesson.

✦

The problem for many people is not that they
think God untrue, but they find him unreal.
It is one thing to believe in God . . .but it
is another thing to experience God as a living
presence. . . God seems so unobtrusive, so
reluctant to proclaim His presence and
availability. If only God would sign some of his
gifts. . .the coloring in the sky. . .
the song of the lark.

✦

Nothing worthwhile is ever realized without
persistence. . . God becomes increasingly real
when we practice His presence wherever we are.

꧁꧂

It may not be difficult to find God in lovely things,
but sooner or later, all of us come to the place where
we must find Him in a difficult or desperate situation.

꧁꧂

Much of modern immorality is not so much badness
as it is confusion over what is right and wrong. . .
Finding our way through a wilderness of ideas toward
acceptable conduct is not an easy assignment. . .
God-centered, intelligent, grounded prayer can
bring us wise guidance. . . (as can asking ourselves)
"are the highest interests of love being served in the
decision that I make and the conduct that follows?"

꧁꧂

A compliment is a gift not to be thrown away
carelessly unless you want to hurt the giver. . .
when someone gives you a complement,
don't disagree or minimize what he says,
for words are gifts too. Accept them gratefully,
even though you don't believe you deserve them.

꧁꧂

No one needs to let (his or her) limitations define
the whole of his or her life.

꧁꧂

How rich are those who learn to receive graciously
and gratefully, for we all receive in a lifetime
more than we are ever able to repay.

＋〜＋

The basis of discipleship is not scholarship,
yet scholarship is important. It is better to have
no ideas relating to religious issues that to entertain
ideas that are unworthy. There is little that is more
dangerous than energized ignorance.

＋〜＋

Each day does offer its own unique gifts, problems
and opportunities . . . It is important to live each day
with a positive perspective. It is not wise to pretend
problems do not exist, but it is wisdom to look
beyond the problem to the possibilities that are in it.

＋〜＋

No person who is fully whole and caring can look out
at our world through dry eyes.

＋〜＋

If we are to make the most of (life) we must give
attention to the development of our spirituality . . .
Enter (life) with joy and enthusiasm. Step into it
with great expectations. Know that no matter what
happens, be it good or evil, you do not go alone.

＋〜＋

Life often presents us with a blank page, and we are at
a loss as to what to put on it. The wisest response is
to keep steadily at the important task at hand and
hope that the story our life tells
will represent our highest possibilities.

✦

In a world of great diversity, there is one thing
we all have in common. Each of us has a handicap
of one kind or another. . . One has this handicap,
and one that. The race of life is run in fetters. We
are inspired and heartened by those who deal
with this human predicament in creative and
courageous ways, turning a minus into a plus and a
disadvantage into an advantage.

✦

We must learn to see each handicap in larger
perspective and not magnify it out of proportion
to what ought to be its inhibiting power.

✦

It is reassuring to know that a person does not
have to be a star to be useful. Giving the support
that enables another to succeed is one of the finest
expressions of humility, love and unselfishness.

✦

Often those who serve in supportive roles
go unheralded, but without them others would not
succeed. . . Most of us will never be famous

or widely known, but it is heartening to know
that no one is useless who encourages and enables
others to realize their best.

✦

At times we must take what yesterday did to us,
or what we did to yesterday and see what we can make
of it today. . . We often must concern ourselves
with the remnants of life.

✦

When we sit in the radius of greatness and wisdom
there is always the possibility
that some of it may rub off on us.

✦

Until we are willing to seek information
from the other side of our social and religious fences,
we cannot begin to lay claim to open-mindedness.

✦

The call, then, is not to less loyalty to our own faith,
but openness to all—a willingness to listen and learn
from others. It is not to point the finger
of judgement but to extend the hand of friendship
and the arms of love.

✦

When we draw closer to one another,
we draw closer to the God who created us all.

✦

It is important early in life to learn how to deal
with disappointment and imperfection
and come to terms with our limitations.

✛

Others find it easier to relate to us
when they see us fail, make mistakes and experience
disappointment. . . our humanness is revealed.

✛

A negative situation is rarely without positive
possibilities provided the loss or imperfection is met
with humility and perspective
and does not kill the spirit of continuing endeavor.

✛

God has implanted deep within the human heart
belief in eternal life . . . we cannot prove its reality
but we are forever trying to prove it—because we
believe in it.

✛

The victory that most of us can win for humanity
will probably not be too glamorous or earth-shaking.
It may simply be faithfulness
in the daily duties that are ours.

✛

If God were small enough to be fully understood,
God would not be big enough to meet our needs.

✛

There is great integrity and common sense
in the willingness to meet with and share in common
venture of service with those
with whom we do not always agree.

+ひ+

We can be true friends of others only as we deliberately
set ourselves to see things as others see them . . .(and)
to work shoulder to shoulder in common enterprise
and to celebrate our differences.

+ひ+

In all controversy the call is not to cast the stone of
judgement or condemnation, but to offer
the helping hand of reconciliation.

+ひ+

We must learn to let go, and to learn how to hold on.
There should by rhythms in life
as there are rhythms in nature, first stress of toil,
and then happy release from it.

+ひ+

The wisest people are those who, although
unrelenting in their quest for answers,
trustingly leave some of the problems
in the hands of God who knows the whole.

+ひ+

Kind words of commendation comprise the most
decorative of all household furnishings.
It is sad in any home if there are
more complaints than compliments.

✦

It is as important to acknowledge a favor
as it is to bestow one.

✦

No one, no matter how famous, is above
the need for affirmation, approval and
words of gratitude.

✦

Finite and limited minds such as ours cannot
be expected to grasp all the mysteries of an infinite
universe or know the whole of God's plan.

✦

It is an art to learn how to win graciously
and it is an art, too, to learn how to lose
without being unduly disheartened or discouraged.

✦

Much of life is larger than we are and was never
intended to be finished.
It is open-ended and ongoing.

✦

Not all who hear have learned to listen.

⌇

Fragmentism is not only inevitable but may have its
essential place in the completed whole. Life is not
made up of one piece, but of many pieces.

⌇

Life on earth is so very brief that many leave it . . .
with hopes and longings unfulfilled and yearnings
unrealized . . . their understanding and conduct,
at best, represent only faint and feeble beginnings.
This dissatisfaction of mere earthly life is what
motivates us to an intimation of something beyond.

⌇

If we listen, we open the door to the possibility
of learning something new. When we speak,
we hear only what we already know.

⌇

The world is moved forward not only by the mighty
shoves of the heroes and the intelligentsia,
but also by the tiny pushes of each honest worker.

⌇

Humans are inclined to hammer away at God, telling
their own plans and wishes and often reserving little
or no time to listen for and understand the plan
of the Supreme Architect. God does not speak
in an audible voice, but sensitive souls by listening

in silence can learn to perceive the Creator's will.

✛

The prerogative of (sympathy and compassion)
need not reside only with God. Each sensitive
human soul sees beneath the masks that others
wear to hide their loneliness, despair and
depression. Each one can heed the words
of the great Scottish writer,
Ian McClaren: " Be kind. Everyone you meet
is carrying a heavy burden."

✛

Sensitive and responsible people have long known
that neutrality is an impossible stance in the presence
of any critical issue. If we do not stand
with the oppressed, we make it easier for the aggressor
to win the day and to continue similar acts
of conquest and oppression.

✛

Prejudices and misunderstandings are often
dissipated when we venture into the home territory
of another person . . . Blessed are those who know
(these) joys, for they shall be continual learners.

✛

It is not impertinence to question doctrines
that seem unwise or untrue. It is a moral
obligation to be as intelligent and informed
in our religion as we can possibly be. . .

Even after conscientious study, it is no disgrace
to feel that we do not have all of the answers . . .
we have stopped learning if we do not feel a little less
informed each day.

༥

Religion at its best is always a marriage of rational
thinking and sound ethical living . . . the seekers
are on a continuous quest to discover religious
conclusions that are emotionally satisfying
and intellectually defensible.

༥

Not to have an awakened conscience, not to be
sensitive to social evils, not to take part in righting
them, not to be active in promoting, establishing
and doing justice — that is heresy. Christianity
is a life before it is a creed.

༥

Prayer is a two way street. We can hear God
answer that there are things that we can do.
There are ways to share . . . the best way
to make glad the heart
of the heavenly Father is to do something
for one of his other children.

༥

It is a sad illusion if we look upon having a strong
faith as something to be considered casually . . .
There comes an hour in every life when everything

seems to have fallen apart . . .
The need for stability and faith at such
an hour is urgent. . . .
Genuine sustaining faith in a time of crisis
need not be an illusion. It comes to those who rest
their faith in God's love and who daily heed the
scripture's counsel: "They who wait upon the Lord
shall renew their strength; they shall mount up
with wings as eagles, they shall run and not be weary,
they shall walk and not faint." Isaiah 40:31

⌇

At the close of our days on earth the question
will not be how much we have,
but how much have we given;
not how much we won,
but how much have we done;
not how much we have saved,
but how much have we sacrificed.

⌇

Perhaps because the word "thanks" is so small
is why it is so often overlooked or considered
unimportant by so many.

⌇

I never cease to be lifted in spirit
by those who stay with it, even though things
are not what they wished they would be.

⌇

The fun of life comes in knowing some useful
purpose yet to be fulfilled. Human life, by its very
nature, needs to be dedicated to something.

+∿+

The best way to aid the cause of evil
is for good men and women to do nothing.

+∿+

It needs to be said as clearly as possible
that no one has been furnished with any
neat formula to answer the question of why one
person suffers more than another . . .
However, God does tell us that everything can
be turned to a positive end
for those who love God.

+∿+

Everything opposed to love, justice and brotherhood,
Jesus declared flatly, is doomed,
for the reason that at the center of the universe
is a God of loving purpose for all people.

+∿+

Jesus was a kind and loving friend to all. He never
met an unimportant person. He wrapped the blanket
of compassion around the poor and dispossessed.
People came to him with their burdens and left
with a new and vital faith in themselves and in God.

+∿+

Jesus never said, "worship me," but he often said,
"follow me" — follow me in the way
of justice, love and kindliness.

ᕗᐤ

Where is God when evil rages? . . .
God revealed great trust in the human family
in granting us freedom — freedom to share in the
process of creation . . . we are called to community,
but we have misused our freedom and have practiced
the arts of selfishness, hostility and enmity
to the vast neglect of the arts of love and peace.

ᕗᐤ

Happiness is the interest that
comes from investing in a life of unselfishness
and service.

ᕗᐤ

The world is moved along not only by the mighty
shoves of its heroes, but also by the aggregate
of tiny pushes of each conscientious citizen.

ᕗᐤ

Conflict and controversy are inevitable in a world
of thoughtful people. Controversy is not only
inevitable, but it is actually desirable . . .
without controversy evils may persist indefinitely.

ᕗᐤ

Our lives are shaped by a series of little thoughts
and activities that make us the persons we become.
Big doors sometimes swing on little hinges.

✦

A large number of small virtues, carefully cultivated,
sacredly guarded and expressed daily, can add up
to a life of integrity and usefulness.

✦

Most of the great advances for humanity
have been made by small groups
moved by great convictions to do great things.

✦

Patience is a quality upon which harmonious
and happy human relations absolutely depend.
A person who lacks it can never hope
to live peacefully with other human beings.

✦

Not only is there wisdom and common sense, but a
large measure of joy and happiness in being patient
and tender with the young; compassionate with the
aged; sympathetic with the striving; and tolerant
with the weak and erring; for sometime in life,
we will have been all of these.

✦

If we start by thinking the ideal is an untroubled life,
then adversity seems a wretched intruder
to be resented . . . but if we start by accepting life as
difficult and tragic, then our blessings, the joy,
beauty and love that enrich us, will appear
so marvelous, it will seem a miracle to have them.

꘡

Adversity, far from being a mere nuisance
or cruelty, is one of the constituent elements
in all great living . . . the pain and trouble we
shrink from, and try to escape, when
used wisely often turn out
to be the source of . . . a new dimension to our
character . . . and (can) add to the joy of living.

꘡

Eternal life is not a postponed affair
which comes only after death. Eternal life
is a way of living that can begin now . . .
Jesus taught that those who were willing to live
this life abundantly and fully according to God's
way of life and service could here and now be
joyfully in the presence of the eternal. There is a
way of living here and now that is deathless.

꘡

Making judgements by censure of others is often
an unconscious attempt to hide our own failings.

꘡

There is the story of a mother who told her children
to divide all people into two classes—friends and
strangers. Friends we love too well to gossip about,
strangers we know too little.

+⌒+

Each life must do some exploring of its own. No one
can live on borrowed faith, and life is a series
of rebirths, not just one. It is a pity to die before we
are ever fully born.

+⌒+

To be a (supporter) is a special gift from God. May
God bless all (supporters)—those who stand behind
the scenes and encourage the good in all of us.

+⌒+

Faith is learning to live with what we do not fully
understand, and faith we must have,
for life is not so simple.

+⌒+

I am not immediately impressed when I am told
that a person has the courage of his convictions.
A bigot can have that. The bigger question is, "Is he
willing to reassess his convictions periodically and
change his mind in the presence of more compelling
logic and common sense?"

+⌒+

Bad habits too weak to be felt
often become too strong to be broken.

+∿+

The world's work does not wait
to be done by perfect people.

+∿+

We can easily understand and forgive a child
who is afraid of the dark. The real tragedy
is the adult who is afraid of the light.

+∿+

There is no dishonor in imperfection. The dishonor
lies in not turning to full account whatever
possibilities do exist. . . Happily, we do not have to be
perfect to make a positive contribution to life.

+∿+

Doubt is one of the most positive words
in our language. . . much that is good has come to us
because someone doubted. . . social (and religious)
progress have turned often on the willingness
of someone to doubt. . . . Doubt was a dimension
of Jesus' life. He was a great believer,
but a magnificent doubter, as well.

+∿+

It is a mark of humility and an eagerness to grow
in our faith when we are willing to live
not only on tenets, but on tentatives.

✦

The truly beautiful people are those whose lives
witness to a strength of character and are therefore
spiritually beautiful . . . They radiate a spiritual
loveliness that refuses to be denied. Without knowing
it, they strengthen us and make the whole world more
beautiful because they dwell within it.

✦

Prejudice damages both the soul of the prejudiced
and the one against whom the prejudice is directed.

✦

When we accept the fact that much of life is hard,
it somehow becomes amazingly easier—easier for us,
and for those around us
who are spared our complaints.

✦

The hard truth is that we have no right to happiness,
per se. . . Life carries no such warranty. . . Those
who set out to pursue happiness seldom find it. . .
For happiness is not a product to be found
but a byproduct of the search.

✦

Happiness comes when we know
that we do not necessarily require happiness.

✦

Being dissatisfied with oneself is the first requisite
of progress. Those who believe they have "arrived"
believe they have nowhere to go. Some not only have
a closed mind to new truth, but they sit on the lid.

✦

There are divine compensations for every
handicap—spiritual resources to help us not only
triumph over handicaps, but also win something
that might not have been possible without them.

✦

Education at its best means liberality of thought
and broadness of view. . . above all, it teaches us
to love and to respect the rights of others,
and to make the world safe for diversity.

✦

We are encouraged to be forgiving
for there is much for which we need to be forgiven.

✦

A failure may be a blessing in disguise. It may mean
self-discovery or a new direction for life.

✦

Being wise and loving in distributing our money
is one of life's highest arts, and yet,
one of its most neglected.

Failure can have a mellowing effect on our lives. Not
much is worse than having to live with a person who
has never failed. . . Those who know the humiliation
of failure are better prepared to forgive others.

Life is a gift to all, but some face it as though
it were a sentence to be served. They die
before they ever fully lived.

Hatred can be like an acid that does more damage
to the vessel in which it is stored than to the object
on which it is poured.

Now and again we need to escape from the inner city
canyons where the sky is cut into narrow ribbons. . .
and look upon the larger world
that God has made. We need to bathe our eyes
in the dew of the morning grass
and wash our minds in the perfumes of the fields.

It is arrogant to relegate to ourselves all knowledge
and to believe that those who differ are in error.
Lovers of liberty must expect and even urge diversity.

꠸

Learning how to disagree agreeably is one of life's
highest arts. . . we are grateful for those
who are willing to hear us out without writing us off.

꠸

A failure simply reveals that something has been
tried. If we have tried to do something and failed,
we are vastly better off than having tried
to do nothing and succeeded.

꠸

It is incumbent on religious people to speak out —
with the humility appropriate to limited vision—
on public issues. But speak they must; or causes held
dear will die by default.

꠸

For in reality, we are responsible not only
for what we do, but for what we do not do.
It's possible to take a false step by standing still.

꠸

We must learn to choose between what is primary
and what is secondary; between what is urgent
and what can wait; between what is of great value
and what is of little consequence. . .

It is wisdom to practice selective procrastination—
putting off indefinitely what we never really
need to do at all.

Taking risks in sharing our convictions
and the controversy that might ensue can be creative
. . . but controversy is not creative if it degenerates
into estrangement, vindictiveness or hatred.

The most human thing we have to do in life
is to learn to speak our honest convictions and
feelings and live with the consequences. This is the
first requirement of love and it makes us vulnerable
to others who may ridicule us. But it is important
to be able to give our vulnerability to others.

In the presence of difference of conclusion,
it is mature to offer a helping hand to reconciliation
. . . to humbly (plan and work) toward wiser decisions
and unconditional love and acceptance.

Religious exclusiveness and blind patriotism
are enemies of the God who created us all. I can
know God within the confines of my own
communion—but only part of God.

(There are heroes who) against all manner of assaults
and disappointments maintain a steady confidence
in God and a belief in God's goodness. . . they lift up
our society and do not lean on it. . . they assume
responsibility for their own lives and try to be helpful
in the lives of others.

✦

There is something worth praise in everyone,
even though it may be undiscovered or not
recognized. . . all people need to be commended
for the good qualities they possess.

✦

It will be a day for celebration when. . .
(the) great religions of the world cease
explaining their differences and begin a search
for elements of the basic unity which could
serve as building blocks for common action and
world accord.

✦

Many people reveal heroism today just in meeting the
challenge of the daily routine. It is often easier
to "mount up with wings as eagles," than it is to "walk
and not faint." Life can become very daily
and it isn't easy to glorify the grind.

✦

There can be no power in the present
if there is no faith in the future.

✢

Generosity is best assessed not by
how much is given but by how much is left after the
gift has been given.

✢

It is better to work for the good
that society was intended to be
than to continually bemoan its shortcomings.

✢

God may not will all that comes to us in the days
ahead, but he will be present to uphold us
and sustain us in whatever experience
will be ours of joy or sorrow.

✢

Reverent agnosticism is not unworthy
in a person of faith. It is wise to admit ignorance
and wait for more light.

✢

It is human foible to blame another
in order to escape the realities of self-blame . . .
we frequently condemn in others our own
temptations and weaknesses. . .
It has been my observation that those
most generous and merciful in judgements of the

faults of others are those who are most free from
faults, themselves.

✦

Listening is a strong creative force . . .
Listening is the language of love. Love permits
a person to think aloud in our presence
without fearing the response of a judgmental
attitude, since listening does not mean we
must agree with all the ideas
another is sharing.

✦

The most humble and helpful people are those who . . .
learn to live with what they do not yet understand,
daily trusting the Creator's love and goodness.

✦

Sensitive people are aware that the world was not
designed for contentment. They see too much
to challenge them, too much important work
to be done, too many changes to be made.

✦

We underrate no religious duty as much as the duty
of being cheerful. The mark of religious people is joy.

✦

Our cup may not run over, but neither is it empty.

✦

The world will be here long after we are gone and
there is only so much each of us can do. To worry
about something we can't help is useless. . . Life is
better and brighter for us and for those around us
if we do not burn up needless energy,
holding the full weight of our anxieties and worries.

There are those who do respond to God's call to . . .
let down their nets into deep waters of concern for
the poor and homeless, or compassion for the rejected
sick and dying and for the many victims of prejudice .
. They shall experience the joy that comes from truly
living life to the full.

We are better able to hang on when we let go
occasionally. Ground that lies fallow becomes more
productive and there are rhythms in the lives
of human beings as well as in nature.

The aim of education is not only the accumulation
of facts and information, but the growing
appreciation of values and worth.

Our deepest need is for community, and those
of harborous spirit are part of life's healing.

Superficial optimists are a peril in serious times.
But a realistic appraisal of life enables us to be aware
of both the evil and the good.

+∿+

What we see depends on what we are looking for.
What we are looking for reveals what we are.

+∿+

Countless acts of kindness and caring go unheralded
each day, but they are real and helpful to many.
Millions of . . . people choose to light a candle
rather than curse the darkness.

+∿+

We may not have people knocking on our door
for shelter, but there are those who are hoping we will
invite them out of a rough and troubling sea
into our harbor of friendship.

+∿+

Anger and all its accompanying moods, including
bad temper, resentment and hostility, can wreck the
health of the body and the mind. They are as likely
to cause disease as a germ. . . . (but) anger in the
form of moral indignation may be the necessary edge
of spiritual vitality. . . Were anger and moral indignation
to die out of the world, society would swiftly rot to
extinction. It is possible to be good–(and) angry!

+∿+

Salute the marathon runner who covers 26 miles, but
reserve the loudest cheers for the man or woman who
stays with (life) against great odds and does not quit
on the hills. On such durable souls the cameras
of heaven are trained. They shall not receive
a perishable wreath, but the greatest prize of all;
the Creator's "well done."

✢

Too many people miss the silver lining
because they expect it to be gold.

✢

Some of life's deepest insights and larger truths are
ushered into our lives by pain and sorrow. . . Again
and again, we come to see that great lives sing most
gloriously when assaulted by the winds of adversity.

✢

A chief source of self-respect, self-discipline,
intellectual power and moral growth is to be
found in one's work. . . . Religious fidelity
can be assessed more realistically and
accurately by the manner in which people
do their work outside the church. . . .
The test of our religion is not only the
way we give our money, but the manner
in which we earn it.

✢

In a world that so readily lauds the "go-getter,"
it is the "go-giver" who most positively
influences our lives.

✦

Each task that contributes to human good is sacred
work . . . No helpful vocation is more sacred than
another. All service ranks the same with God.

✦

The light of God's love can shine through
each individual's life at the point where that life
is lived and that work done, no matter how great
or insignificant the task may be.

✦

To mark spiritual growth, there can be questions,
which when answered honestly, give us a sense
of the direction in which we are moving. Do I have
a greater awareness of God . . . have I changed my
mind recently . . . am I seeking answers to new
questions . . . does my life reflect the joy that my
religious faith should bring . . . do I live each day
in an attitude of gratitude . . . have I overcome any
needless worries . . . do I do something for someone
else each day at some cost to myself . . . do I harbor
resentment and grudges or am I always ready
to forgive . . . do I have any unfinished tasks?

✦

Humility and courage are revealed when we are
intolerant of the evils that plague our own lives—
complacency, indifference, selfishness, apathy,
procrastination and a host of other ills
that invade our lives and deny us the fullness
and usefulness our Creator intended.

✦

Many people today, loyal to their own high ideals,
walk toward the light of justice, honor and truth,
and the shadow of good influence falls behind them.
They attract rather than compel others
toward goodness.

✦

We all have a shadow of influence that follows us
wherever we go. For good or ill it falls on others.
Silently, it reaches where we are not aware,
and often touches those we had not intended.

✦

It is wise to recognize that, at best, we can have
only a partial understanding of God . . . It requires
eternity to know infinity. But the partialness
of our knowing must not discourage us in our quest
(of knowing God).

✦

In the presence of problems and perplexities,
no merit exists in adopting an attitude of gloom and
doom. We tend to become like that which we believe

ourselves to be . . . we never build anything up
by continually tearing it down . . . we should start
with the realization of the good we already have . . .
see the problems . . .but see the possibilities too.

✦

Jesus taught that God's love is as international
as the sun and as all-encompassing as the rain that
falls on the just and the unjust. It knows no
boundaries of race, class or nationality.

✦

To see life as given to us by a loving God,
is to know that life is invested with deathless meaning
and invincible dignity.

✦

It is wise and humble to at least be open to voices
other than those we usually hear . . . to listen does
not mean automatic acceptance, but it opens
the door to the possibility of learning.

✦

We cannot be certain that others will respond to us
in love — that we cannot control. But we do have the
power to love, and in that loving we can find deep
fulfillment, even if love is rejected.

✦

The great message of Christmas for the world
is that God is in it. God did not create the world and
then go away and leave it. We live and move
and have our being in God's presence.

+∿+

The virus of prejudice that plagues and weakens our
culture will not die of itself. It must be continually
subjected to the great light
of the oneness of humanity.

+∿+

Let us sing, dance and rejoice in the great truths
that give life purpose and meaning and enable us
to live with dignity and joy, knowing that we are
always, in life or death, in God's presence,
God's love and God's care.

+∿+

Words are gifts too . . . gentle words fall lightly,
but bear much weight.

+∿+

No good point is served by looking to the past and
regretting its failures—missing the joys
of the present and the possibilities of tomorrow.

+∿+

One liability of any age is that we might sleep
through great change, failing to achieve the
new attitudes and actions that new situations

demands. . . . It is a mark of mature society
that it can accept constructive change.
There is no merit in clinging to outmoded
concepts and unaccepted injustices . . .

༺༻

Success is never automatic. Self-discipline and
determination, and above all,
persistence and perseverance are required.

༺༻

It should be liberating to know that we do not
have to know everything. Half of being smart
is knowing what we do not know.

༺༻

There are mysteries that can be made
plain to us, perhaps, only in the
clearer light of another world.

༺༻

Great minds and great spirits are society's most
valuable assets . . . because everything we say
and do is the length and shadow of our
own souls, our influence is determined
by the quality of our being.

༺༻

The work of the spirit is never done.
Our spirituality is a process.

ᆉ

Do something each day for someone else
at some cost to yourself.

ᆉ

It is unfortunate, if in our hurry to make a living,
we have no time to pause and make a life.

ᆉ

The game of life is much like a game of cards.
We must play what is dealt us,
and the glory consists not so much in winning
as in playing an imperfect hand well.

ᆉ

Not to choose is to choose.

ᆉ

Each of us has to live with himself or herself every day
and so it is essential to furnish the mind
in a way that will assure . . . a mind filled
with positive and loving thoughts.

ᆉ

Neutrality is impossible. We are either for an idea
or a cause, or we are against it. No one is
an innocent bystander. We are inextricably linked

in one body of humanity. What happens anywhere
happens everywhere, and what happens to anyone
happens to everyone.

✦

No matter how depraved or dissipated humans may
sometimes be, they are still God's children—loved and
accepted. Everyone is someone—someone divine.

✦

We discover who we are
when we commit our lives to God and live God's way
of unconditional love for all.

✦

Argument is the longest distance between two points.

✦

One reason for our inability to achieve simplicity
is that we clutter our lives with more (material) things
than we actually need. . . .   The quest for the simple
life is further deterred by our having built
an altar to energy and made activity our God. . .
We need time to be still—to sit, to observe, to reflect,
to absorb, to enjoy, to learn . . . (to put) off
indefinitely what (we) never really need to do at all.

✦

Truth never needs to fear the light.

✦

No one is perfect, but everyone possesses some good,
even lovable traits. This lovability
needs to be recognized and fed.

+∽+

The biggest disservice to ourselves and to others
is to have a good impulse to commend someone,
and then, to remain silent.

+∽+

Mysterious though it is, the characteristics in human
nature which we love best grow in soil which contains
a strong mixture of handicap and trouble.

+∽+

Finding a way to live the simple life
is one of life's complications.

+∽+

Even when a sin in not known, it is known
to the transgressor, and it affects the way this person's
life is lived . . . but the joys and breadth
of possibilities of a full and productive life,
which are available to those not hampered
by misdeeds are limitless.

+∽+

All we have to do is live, and the influence of our lives
will follow us as surely as our shadows.

+∽+

The life of a whole community is sometimes
transformed in its ideals and aims by a person
who has never thought of posing as an influence
or setting an example. But the way this person goes
is the way others want to follow.

✦

We may long to accomplish great and noble tasks.
But it is possible to do the humble, mundane tasks
of every day as though they were great and noble.

✦

Great ability is important.
But God is not so much interested in
our ability as in our availability—the will
to do what we can.

✦

Half of achieving anything
is knowing what we have to give up to get it.

✦

There is magic in a word of praise.

✦

Hearts often pine away in secret
for want of kindness and encouragement.

✦

Revenge degrades all who tolerate its presence
in their minds and hearts. A vengeful spirit should

be condemned not only because it can lead
to harming the offender, but because it also harms
the one who harbors the grudge.

+∽+

Money is an extension of our own personalities . . .
the use we make of it determines the ends
our lives will serve.

+∽+

The deepest need of the human spirit is community —
common unity — good will and acceptance.

+∽+

It is wise and magnanimous to never let any critical
word or malevolent act maneuver us out of the orbit
of unconditional love, acceptance and good will.

+∽+

How do we believe in a good and loving God
in a world where evil rages and there is so much
suffering and sorrow . . ? Why some suffer more
than others, we do not pretend to know.
But by recognizing God's gifts, God's sense of order,
God's moral, physical and spiritual laws—
and by faith made strong and firm in remembering
God's goodness—we are empowered to meet
the evils and sorrows we encounter.

+∽+

The greatest of all faults is to be conscious of none.

ᕽᏔᏍ

The ability to transmute a hindrance into an end
is one of the most beneficent gifts of God and one
of the greatest of all human achievements . . . We are
strong when we can make our weakness our strength.

ᕽᏔᏍ

It is a mark of humility and gratitude to be aware
that someone has paid a price for every good thing
that is ours.

ᕽᏔᏍ

How easy it is to give that which costs us nothing.

ᕽᏔᏍ

The sturdiest faith has always come out of the struggle
with doubt . . . people of faith are people of doubt.

ᕽᏔᏍ

Nothing worthwhile or creative
is accomplished in a crowd.

ᕽᏔᏍ

Suffering and sorrow . . . remain the supreme
mystery of life. A great source of steadiness
can be found in the knowledge that countless others
have faced precisely the same problems without being
utterly defeated in spirit. . . . No wound of the body
or soul is unique or entirely new, and others

with similar scars have something to say to us . . .
Among the sources of human strength is a resource
unequaled—the friendship of any person who has
preceded another through a similar valley
who can quietly say, "I understand."

✢

We can all be gracious receivers and it is as important
to know how to receive a gift as it is to bestow one.

✢

If I do ask myself, "why me?" as I am assaulted by
(hardship and sorrow,) I must also ask, "why me?"
about my blessings.

✢

It is a mark of faith, nobility and courage
to turn a minus into a plus and to discover positive
good in the midst of greatest sorrow.

✢

How rich we are if we know how to receive graciously,
for all of us receive in our lifetime
more than we are ever able to return.

✢

Sometimes when I consider the
tremendous consequences that follow
from little things—a chance word, a letter, a call,
a tap on the shoulder—I am tempted to think
there are no little things. . .   The good life is the

computation of many littles—acts of honor,
kindness, thoughtfulness and love. . .
For a life can be made or broken
by such as these—little things.

❧

Growth in faith is a continuing process of rebirth
and growth. The tragedy of life is that many die
before they are fully born.

❧

Prejudice builds walls of separation . . .
we were created for community . . .
(and) anyone who breaks down walls of
prejudice and alienation and builds bridges
to unify is a great human benefactor.

❧

Our days are as the shadows that fly across the sunny
hill. The years pass swiftly . . . (this) can be a call
to give priority to values of worth in the brief days
allotted to us. . . Death is a part of life,
and is not devoid of positive contributions . . .
the presence of death
makes more meaningful all of the values of life.

❧

Love of self is an important . . . teaching because
people cannot live amicably with others unless they
can live amicably with themselves. . . (not the) kind
of love that sets self above others, but the kind of love

that appreciates our own best gifts
and determines to make something of them
in order to give the best to others.

✢

Man's inhumanity to man makes countless thousands
mourn. The challenge is to conduct ourselves
so that we are part of the answer
and not part of the problem.

✢

So many of the tragedies of life seem meaningless
and unnecessary. Yet with the responsible use of the
brain the Creator gave us we come to conclusions
that enable us to believe in the rationality
of the world and the love and goodness of God.

✢

The world lies in proportion to the number
of ordinary people who . . . have such intense pride
and love for themselves that they will permit
in themselves no bigotry, prejudice or dishonor . . .
they will not permit a lesser self to lay claim
to the only life they have to live.

✢

People may not be greatly swayed by our thoughts,
but they can be deeply moved by our thoughtfulness.

✢

A Christian's "Cross" is not his or her own cross. It
is the voluntary acceptance of another's burdens,
or identification with worthy causes . . . The heaviest
cross Jesus carried was not the wooden one he bore
to his crucifixion, but bearing the burdens of the
poor, the hungry, the dispossessed and oppressed.

+~+

The highest art of a human's life is the ability
to empathize with the joys and sorrows of others.

+~+

An important challenge is to discover one's best self
and nurture it so that it dominates one's life.

+~+

We may not be able to take away
another person's grief and pain, but we may share it.

+~+

Most of us, at one time or another, have wished to be
someone else . . . and yet God does not want us to be
someone other than the person we are . . . you were
meant to be yourself at your best.

+~+

There should be a rhythm in human life,
as there is rhythm in all of nature; first, stress of toil,
and then happy release from it.

+~+

Heaven begins on Earth for those who are unselfish
and caring . . . who live with a consciousness
of God's continuing presence. Eternal life is not a
postponed affair that comes after death. It is a way of
living in this world . . . (that) says that life is endless
and unconquerable.

✦

It is a mark of humility and maturity to know how
dependent we are . . . As we grow in our recognition
of our interdependence we deepen our gratitude
for what others have contributed to our welfare.

✦

The life of an entire community is sometimes
transformed for good . . . by those who have never
thought of posing as a good influence . . . but (who)
have simply gone on living in an elevating way
that others want to follow.

✦

Humility is the foundation of all other virtues.
To be humble is to be teachable.

✦

No one can find greater joy than that which comes
from taking a barren, desolate and unpromising plot
of life and making something productive
and beautiful—something that would never have been
except for our effort.

✦

We can all be channels through whom God's power
can flow. It is not necessary that we have prestige,
power, position, beauty, or wealth.

+∿+

The entire universe is God's classroom
and we are all called to be continual learners.

+∿+

We can easily understand and forgive a child
who is afraid of the dark, but the real tragedy
is an adult who is afraid of the light.

+∿+

Those who love are lifted above enmity
and vindictiveness. They are set free
from the burden of grudges and hatreds.
A Christians' "Cross" is not his or her own cross.
It is the voluntary acceptance of another's burdens,
or identification with worthy causes . . . The heaviest
cross Jesus carried was not the wooden one he bore
to his crucifixion, but bearing the burdens of the
poor, the hungry, the dispossessed and oppressed.

+∿+

Life is not all velvet. Some of it is sandpaper.
God puts thorns on rose bushes.

+∿+

The hard truth is we have no right to happiness . . .
Those who set about to pursue happiness

seldom find it . . .   A person has the highest prospect
for happiness who makes God sovereign in life,
seeks to do the Creator's will and desires
more to serve than to be served.

+ひ+

We can never be sure what effect our prayers have
on others, but we do know what our prayers
for others do for us . . . (our) ties of love with them
are strengthened . . . we feel closer to them
and become more caring.

+ひ+

God gave us a backbone to bear our ills,
but God gave us a funny bone, as well.

+ひ+

We cannot be sure whether our prayers have any effect
on those with whom we differ, but we do know
that our prayers can drive animosities from our own
lives and bring inner peace.

+ひ+

Laughter is God's hand
on the shoulder of a troubled world.

+ひ+

The two great enemies of humanity are blind
patriotism and religious exclusiveness.

+ひ+

No religion has all the truth. We have much to learn
from one another.

Set out to do something for someone each day
at some cost to oneself.

No amount of piety on the Sabbath
can atone for a crooked deal on Wednesday.

People are just as religious whether they make soap
or sermons . . . all workers who do useful work
with faithfulness and honesty (do) sacred tasks.

Were moral indignation to die out of the world,
society would swiftly rot to extinction.

A positive personality sees some good
even in compromising situations. The following sign
reads: "Lost dog. Has 3 legs. Blind in left eye, missing right ear, tail broken. Answers to LUCKY."

Weaknesses can become incentives
to greater achievement.

We are all handicapped in one way or another . . .
a person is foolish not to be what he can be
simply because he can't be what he wants to be.

꒦

The manner in which we handle life's problems
determines the quality of our days. Adversity can
make or break people depending on . . . how it is
directed. Even those who are infirm can minister
greatly to those who nurse and care for them,
through the gift of gratitude, good cheer and a spirit
of optimism and joy.

꒦

In a world which . . . sometimes seems to be falling
apart, we need to center our attention on the eternal
things that abide . . . unchanged—truth, justice,
righteousness, love, compassion and courage.
These are like fixed stars.

꒦

We do not serve God or humans in general.
We serve in particular.

꒦

When we surrender to God's will of divine love;
self-fulfillment and public usefulness is found.
This is what it means to be saved.

꒦

We are given only enough glimpses of God
and the pattern God is weaving to sustain faith
and make us yearn for that nearer presence
and larger knowledge which is eternal life.

✦

We are not always free to choose what will happen
to us, but we are free to choose what our response
will be . . . we can respond angrily (or we can) say,
"What can we find here to be thankful for?" Our
attitude determines whether we are victim or victor.

✦

Two very important days in every life are
the day we are born and the day when we know
why we were born.

✦

It is a pity if a person comes to the time to die,
only to discover that he never really lived.

✦

People can achieve meaning in their lives
only if they have made a commitment
to the development of their own highest possibilities,
a commitment to loved ones and a commitment
to the divine power beyond themselves.

✦

God has implanted deep within the human soul
the belief in eternal life . . . to believe in immortality

is the supreme act of faith
in the reasonableness of God.

✦

An intelligent response to life is to find something
positive in each new day.

✦

Even though we may have . . .
a host of friends, we are forced, in a certain sense, to
lead a lonely life. We all have days when we must
come to terms with ourselves.

✦

The good news of the Gospel is that the club is still
open to membership. It is not a private, exclusive
group. "Whoever will, may come."

✦

It is the spirit of love and acceptance of diversity
that must be nurtured. Such a spirit, tolerant,
gracious and charitable, offers a basis for happy
and harmonious community life. Barriers that
separate people must be fashioned into bridges.
Enemies must become friends.

✦

To be able to laugh at ourselves
is a sign of wholeness and wholesomeness.

✦

One of the great reliefs of life
is to discover one's own mediocrity.

+∿+

There are possibilities for creative and constructive
replenishment of body, mind and spirit
when we listen . . . when we are still
we stand the chance of learning something.

+∿+

What we are born with is God's gift to us.
What we do with it is our gift to God and humanity.

+∿+

How we handle the adversities with which we are
confronted determines the quality of our lives.
Adversity is neutral; it can make or break us,
however, depending on how we face and handle it.

+∿+

You are a factor in every situation.
Never discount your own importance in the struggle
to make a better world. We may never occupy
positions of high importance nor directly influence
dramatic decisions, but if we are faithful with what we
have, where we are, there will never come an end
to the good that we have done.

+∿+

.

There would be very little love given
if people gave only as much love to their neighbors
as many give to themselves.

꩜

One life can make a difference—and a great
difference. Each day, each one of us leaves behind
a little legacy of helpfulness or harm.

꩜

One of the chief challenges confronting all of us
is to stay alive as long as we live.

꩜

I may hope that in taking note of the mistakes
of others, I might be wise enough to correct my own.

꩜

A common ailment of our day
is premature formation of opinion . . . many start
out intent on discovering the world of truth, but they
settle down on the first little island of knowledge,
build a fortress and shoot down any idea
that threatens their security.

꩜

Asking for all things that we might enjoy life,
we are given life that we might enjoy all things.

꩜

One way or another, transgressions do come to light.
And although God can forgive the sin,
God cannot remove the consequences.

+∿+

What do we make, then, of men who are religiously
unorthodox . . . but in behavior sometimes come
close to saintliness? God is in no way obligated
to live only where people look for God. God often
appears where we least expect to find God–and in the
most unlikely people. . . The faithful expect God
to do the unexpected and wise men
and women know . . . to look for the Eternal
where others would scarcely think to look.

+∿+

The years teach much that the days don't know.
A Christians' "Cross" is not his or her own cross.
It is the voluntary acceptance of another's
burdens, or identification with worthy causes . . .
The heaviest cross Jesus carried was not the
wooden one he bore to his crucifixion, but
bearing the burdens of the poor, the hungry,
the dispossessed and oppressed.

+∿+

Even though everyone wants to live a long time,
nobody wants to be old.

+∿+

To be successful one has to be able to:
Do one's duty even when one is not watched.
Keep at the job until it is finished.
Make use of criticism without letting it whip you.
Bear injustice without retaliating.
See the evil in the world, yet be ready
to believe the best about others.

✦

People are never more insecure than when they
become obsessed with their fears at the expense
of their dreams, or when the ability to fight becomes
more important than the things worth fighting for.

✦

It is wise to recognize that we have, at best, only a
partial understanding of God . . . it requires eternity
to know infinity. It is really better to have no
opinion (of God) than one that is unworthy.
Even though everyone wants to live a long time,
nobody wants to be old.

✦

All of us must make several important connections
if ours is to be a live and vital life . . it is advisable
to keep connections with our own best selves . . .
with our own best physical selves . . . with our best
mental selves, with the best thoughts and the best
books . . . with the Bible . . . with family and friends
. . . with our work . . . with God who gave us life.

✦

Good friends are real joys of life . . . reaching out
to others can become a way of life. People are lonely
when they build walls instead of bridges.

❦

Work is one way an individual makes a contribution
to our world. It is in work that religious convictions
find expression . . . that personalities are shaped and
faith is nurtured. Even work that is humble and may
seem relatively unimportant may be a window
through which divine light can shine.

❦

Sensitive persons are open to truth regardless
of its origin or source.

❦

One of the most perplexing and frustrating aspects
of life is the sense of incompleteness
and fragmentalism that characterizes many of our
days . . . there is hope however, when we realize that
incompleteness is essential in a rational view of life
as a whole. . . It is not always what people actually
accomplish that most accurately defines them.
It can also be what they are trying to do and be—the
goals for which they aspire, the hopes and yearnings
that are theirs.

❦

Life is not made up of great sacrifices and duties,
but of little things in which smiles and kindness and

small obligations, given daily, are what win the heart
and reveal what is real and good. . . Those who
inspire us are the generous souls who pour out their
lives without measuring. They give more than they
have to and take less than they deserve.

+↻+

The story of history is, in large measure, the story
of men and women who have overcome great odds,
surmounted failures and made a significant
contribution to life even in the presence of defeat.

+↻+

One slip doesn't mean we are forever a sinner any
more than one good deed makes us forever a saint.

+↻+

Many positive values can evolve out of failure. It can
have a mellowing effect on our lives . . . to know a
few failures can help make a person fit to live with.

+↻+

A society is continuously recreated for good or ill
by its members.

+↻+

Kindness has great transforming power. . . Outward
appearances are often deceiving. A smiling person
may be nursing a deep hurt . . . Be kind.

+↻+

No one of us is entire in himself or herself.
Our family and our friends are the rest of us. We
need others to find our own deepest fulfillments.

꩜

Worship in order to restore the balance of life
and permit the message of God—
which is often unheard in the whirlwind of life,
to be heard in the still, small voice of calm.

꩜

One of the marks of greatness is the ability
to be able to see potential greatness in others.

꩜

It is amazing that some otherwise sensible people
have a way of seeing . . . only the problem
and not the promise.

꩜

Prayer is not a way of getting
God to do what we want, but a way of putting ourselves in such a relationship with God that God can
do—in, for and through us— what God wants.

꩜

The deepest need is to be loved, the greatest thing
we can do for another is to love that person.

꩜

It is love that sees the possibilities in others . . . love
calls into being what is hidden, but nonetheless real.
Goodness may be only in the embryonic stage,
but love can bring it fully alive . . . there is goodness
in everyone. It remains only to be discovered.

❧

You can't touch a sugared doughnut
without getting some sugar on your fingers. And
(therefore) it leaves a trail of sweetness wherever it
goes . . . it would be a better world if somehow we
could be like sugared doughnuts—leaving a trail
of flavorful joy and fragrance behind us. . . Wouldn't
it be great if everyone who had contact with us felt a
little happier because their lives had touched ours?

❧

One of God's greatest gifts—
perhaps the greatest gift—to each of us is being born
into an unfinished world and given a share with God
in creation. We become worthy of this great trust
when we commit our lives to the Creator's way of
unconditional, non-manipulative, all-accepting love.

❧

It is not enough simply to believe in God. It is
commitment to the Creator's will
that gives integrity to our faith. Religion is behavior
and not mere belief.

❧

It is incongruous to hold malice in our hearts
when we are on our knees . . . praying.

᚛

There are no hopeless situations. There are only
those who have grown hopeless about them . . .
There are always things we can do to make life
brighter and better for others. It may not be the
project for which we had hoped or been trained.
It may seem commonplace and simple,
but it can be very important.

᚛

Can we follow Jesus today? Yes, we can. It may be
we follow stumblingly and inadequately, but the call
to follow is worth our effort to respond, for to follow
is to discover the deeper joys and greater usefulness
God would have us know.

᚛

Prayer is the conscious attempt
to become aware of the presence of God.

᚛

In prayer comes the realization that we are not alone.
We are in God's hands. When we sense more of
God's love and caring, we rise above our fears . . .
Our central protection against fear is faith in the love
and goodness of God.

᚛

Grief, like trouble, is never
welcome . . . but once it comes it can be
transmuted and channeled into service and sympathy,
into understanding and undergirding of others.
In all things, God can work for good.

✦

We need a sense of humor to get along with others. . .
to be able to laugh at ourselves is a sign of wholeness
and wholesomeness . . . To see our inconsistencies,
mistakes, tempers and scorn for others
keeps our egos in proper perspective.

✦

One of life's chief joys is to take an unpromising
situation and work to create something beautiful
where nothing beautiful has ever been.

✦

We are all less than we wish we were. None of us ever
arrives. We are always in the process of becoming.
But we all need encouragement in the good we do.

✦

The needed lesson in life is to learn how to meet
and deal with danger—not how to avoid danger.

✦

Little things are heroic
because so many fail to do them.

✦

Trouble is not necessarily an intruder. There are
times when a detour means a better road to follow.
Everything will not be perfect in this life, and we
ought not to expect it to be.

†∿†

Greatness is nearby in many people if we have the eyes
to see it . . . unheralded heroes and heroines
who have forsaken their own plans and pleasure
to care for an invalid wife or husband, parent or
child. . . there are single parents . . . there are those
who walk on streets who are veterans of mental health
wars . . . there are those who didn't quite make it in
the corporate race for the roses . . . . Others dwell in
bodies of pain, twisted and deformed
by disease . . . . The world is not devoid of heroes
and heroines . . . we see them around us every day.
They will not often capture the attention
of the media or be recipients of medals or plaques,
but they deserve to be saluted. . . .

†∿†

The contribution of Christian faith
to the problem of evil has lain not so much
in supplying a theory to explain it as in furnishing
a power to surmount it, and it gives us faith
that assures us that no matter how adverse conditions
may seem to be, we are always in God's care.

†∿†

Often those who do the most good are . . . those who,
like a fully laden apple tree, are so rich in their own
spiritual fruitage that no one can brush against them
without bringing down something good to eat.

✦

When we follow duty, we enter into life . . .
duty is not our chain, but our release—a release into
competent, joyful and useful living. . . Duty is
the very condition of abundant living.

✦

The reward for a job well done
is being the one who did it.

✦

Love is expressed by overlooking
the faults or mistakes of another.

✦

When we try to carry the responsibilities of a lifetime
all at one moment, it is overpowering and we fail.
But day by day builds a pattern of victory.

✦

People are not coerced into goodness, they are lured
into it by attractive, radiant and joyful personalities.

✦

Those who know no hardships will know
no hardihood. Adversity, far from being a mere

nuisance or cruelty, is one of the constituent
elements in all great living and is to be finely
and constructively used.

҉

It is the recognition that all people carry with them
some sorrows and pain that encourages us
to be thoughtful with all.

҉

In the rush, hurry and tension of life today, it is
important to develop the habit of taking time—of
making time—to be quiet, to listen, be still and grow.

҉

Those who can change the focus of their
concentration from themselves to others, losing
themselves in seeking the well-being and happiness
of others, may without knowing it, do something
of great value and importance for themselves. They
compensate for their problems by forgetting
themselves and discover the profound truth that
"whosoever will save his life shall lose it and
whosoever will lose his life shall find it."

҉

Love is the doorway through which the human soul
passes from selfishness to service, from solitude and
loneliness to kinship with all humankind.

҉

There are many people in our world today who are
hurting, plagued with physical or mental ills, marital
incompatibilities, financial problems,
or one or more of the many problems that afflict
human beings. They need to know that someone
cares about them. They need to hear our love.

✥

We need to let the tides of God's love move
into our lives so that we may go forth better able
to cope with life's problems.

✥

It is not what happens to us, but what happens in us,
that supremely counts. Whenever we conquer
our own fears and failures, whenever we do with love
and courage the thing we have to do, then no matter
what the result may seem to be at the moment,
we are victorious and are counted
as those who are successful in the eyes of God.

✥

The good life is marked by countless little extra deeds
of love and helpfulness done throughout each day.
When we extend ourselves and do the extras
that are open to us, we make it a brighter, better,
more loving world.

✥

To affirm the goodness we see
in others breaks down alienation and makes firm

friendships. The gift of affirmation or praise is one
of the best gifts we can give to another.

❧

Although we may not be great ourselves, we can make
one of life's greatest contributions by encouraging
the greatness in others.

❧

People are fools to not be what they can be,
simply because they can't be what they
would like to be.

❧

People may not be greatly swayed by our thoughts,
but they can be deeply moved by our thoughtfulness.

❧

The salvation of the world depends on men
and women who will take the risk
of facing ill will with goodwill, people who will try
to break the vicious cycle of evil.

❧

Ours is a day when the simplicities
of love and caring must come center stage.
Everywhere in our society people are bleeding
to death spiritually and emotionally.
The tourniquet of love and caring must be applied.

❧

What we see in our society depends on what we are looking for. What we are looking for reveals what we are. What we are depends on what we think in our hearts and what we do with our hands.

༄

We should not expect to find friends without faults, for we ourselves are not without faults.

༄

We give evidence of compassion and sensitivity when we strive to see beneath the masks others wear to hide their hurt. . . . What better use of our lives could there be than to bring light and hope into a world that for so many people is dark and hopeless.

༄

We tend to measure our success in life by the wrong yardstick. The question is not so much what we achieve as what we become. What do both success and failure do to us?. . . . The important thing is that we have learned through it all— patience, humility, tenderness, compassion and an utter dependence upon God.

༄

Life will be easier when we learn that it is hard. Adversity can elicit talents which in prosperous circumstances would have lain dormant.

༄

No doubt the pessimist and the optimist eventually
end up in the same place, but the optimist
has more fun getting there.

✢

The real measure of life is not our successes but our
goals. And it is not alone what people do that exalt
them, but what they are trying to do.

✢

It is wise for us to learn to forgive others because we
have so much for which to be forgiven. Those who
cannot forgive others break the bridge over which all
must travel, and the bridge must be strong.

✢

The greatest sin we can commit against ourselves
is having a good impulse and never acting upon it.

✢

The real heroes in life are those who refuse
to let discouragement defeat them.

✢

Adversity teaches many lessons
that we can learn no other way.

✢

It is important to know that success
in God's eyes is not what we achieve, but what the

process of the struggle does to us—
not where we are, but what we are.

✢

Love is the most powerful force in the world.

✢

There is a yearning to rediscover elemental
things—things that are honest and basic to life.

✢

Reading is one of the most
positive ways to use the mind, and the love of books
is the doorway through which we enter into the purest
and most perfect pleasure God has prepared for us.

✢

Whatever affects one directly affects all indirectly.
We must be unrelenting in our quest for peace.

✢

The message that God attached to (Jesus') invincible
life is . . ."to anybody who (discovers) this,
I love you."

✢

We cease to grow and our conclusions become fixed
at a point where we cease asking questions.

✢

People do not believe in immortality
because they have proved it, but they are forever
trying to prove it because they believe it.

✦

It is interesting to note that books often show us
that the original thoughts we thought were ours
are really not very new at all.

✦

We are inspired by people who have the gift
of being able to translate difficult situations
into positive gains—those who turn a negative
into a positive and do not simply grin and bear it,
but do something, which makes them better
than they would otherwise have been.

✦

About the Author

Reverend Doctor Dale Turner, who began his career as a minister in Michigan in 1943, never stepped inside a church until he was 18. His parents were of different denominations—Catholic and Protestant—and so solved their dilemma by not going to church.

Dr. Turner attended West Virginia Wesleyan, a Methodist college, because of its athletic program—he had intended to become a high school football coach. Upon graduating, he had a choice between two graduate school scholarships—one for a master's degree in physical education at Columbia University, and the other, which he accepted, to Yale Divinity School.

Dr. Turner spent 10 years in Lawrence, Kansas, teaching at the University and preaching at the Plymouth Congregational Church. He moved to Seattle in 1958 to lead the University Congregational Church.

He retired in 1982 and began writing a weekly column for the Religion page of the Seattle Times, which he still writes today.

Dr. Turner lives in Seattle with his wife of more than 50 years, Leone. They have four sons, three daughters-in-law, six grandsons, and two granddaughters.